The Emerald Mountain

The Emerald Mountain

by

Jeanne A. O'Donnell

RoseDog Books

PITTSBURGH, PENNSYLVANIA 15222

ISBN # 0-8059-9213-8
Printed in the United States of America

First Printing

For additional information or to order additional books, please write:
Rosedog Publishing
701 Smithfield Street
Pittsburgh, Pennsylvania 15222
U.S.A.
1-800-834-1803
Or visit our web site and on-line bookstore at www.rosedog.com

To Jeshua of Nazareth

Contents

Come, Let Us Sit on the Log Again .1

The Emerald Mountain 2

Credo 3

From The Angels 4

Music of the Spheres 5

Nightlights 6

Star Seed: Look at the Star's Silvery Light 7

The End Times 8

Ammachi 9

Star Seed: Crystal Caves of Healing 10

Star Seed: Poetry from the White Light 11

Life Cycles 12

Bimini 13

September 11, 2001 15

Children of God 16

Eternal Now 17

Star Seed: I Hear Your Yearning .18

Star Seed: I Have a Spider on my Wall 19

The Separation from God 20

Star Seed: A Perfect Nighttime 21

Kid Stuff 22

Star Seed: Lives of Bliss Replace Longing and Strife 23

Star Seed: Have You Listened to the Wind 24

Star Seed: "I've Come to Express My Love for You" 25

Star Seed: Cry for the Children 26

Star Seed: We Can Heal Ourselves 27

Beaches 28

Star Seed: The Great Spirit of the Monolith 29

Meditation with the Dolphins 30

Star Seed: The Night Watches 31

The Flutemaker 32

Star Seed: Angels Are Wonderful Things 33

Star Seed: If I Dip My Cup 34

Star Seed: There Are Starving People 35

Star Seed: Help Each Other 36

Creation 37

Genesis 38

Magic 39

A Note From The Author

Two years ago I had the pleasure of attending a class offered by a woman who channels angels. During one channeling class it was sugggested that we take a pen and paper and write down whatever we were inspired to write. Frankly, I had my doubts that I would be able to write anything, inspired by angels or otherwise.

However, I did what was suggested and to my suprise words began to stream through my mind taking me back to my early meditations many years ago. The result of that evening's attempt is the first poem in this collection "Come let us sit on the log again."

After, I had only to sit down with my pen and paper and the words would flow. I hope I have pleased the angels whom I love and revere.

Introduction

I climbed the side of the mountain unaware of its beautiful symbolism. From rock to rock I took my baby steps and when I grew tired or if I stumbled a strong hand was placed under my arm.

I searched the path behind and the path ahead to see the face of the supporter of my quest but none was there. And still I climbed for with each foot placed one in front of the other a vision appeared in my mind and I was transported back to the valley where my journey began.

Jesus sat on a fallen tree waiting for me as I walked toward him through scrub grass and wild flowers. A narrow road of dirt and stones stretched from our meeting place, for indeed it became that, and led to the base of the mountain in the distance. When the time and the messages were appropriate we would walk on the road hand in hand while questions were asked by me and answered by Jesus to the level of my understanding and the evolution of my spirit.

He appeared one day while I was in deep meditation and approached me leading a handsome black horse. He suggested that I get on the horse and ride and he would hold the reins while we walked along the road beside a stream bubbling and singing its watery tones of joy in being a part of life.

Communication became mind to mind as we traveled slowly along; he always anticipating my queries and answering me with great patience; sometimes seriously, sometimes humorously, always with great wisdom and love.

As we progressed and shortened the distance between the fallen tree and the mountain my sweet-tempered horse changed from black to grey to pure, glistening white.

We arrived at a little footbridge spanning the water of life and from this footbridge a clearer and wider path led to the base of the mountain. I was to cross the bridge and continue my journey unescorted, but never alone. I dismounted and thanked my four-legged friend and my beloved guide and walked toward the mountain to start my climb.

Come, Let Us Sit on the Log Again

Come, let us sit on the log again; see our mountain,
see how far we've come from the white horses
and the black horses.
Hold my hand as we walk toward the peak,
over the bridge, over the water of life.
We walk past Lazarus in his tetrahedron.
We climb hand in hand up the crystal staircase
as we did many times before.
Go alone now; climb, climb, climb into the arms of God.
He waits for you with unimaginable love.

The Emerald Mountain

The Emerald Mountain,
that divine place of healing and knowledge,
which every soul aspires to climb,
whose counterpart lies under the cosmic sea,
will one day rise from its salty grave.
All will enter at its base
to climb the inside tiers of ramps and rays.
Healing color and golden nuggets of wisdom
bathe its climbers as they ascend its sides
to the apex of perfection, and are expelled upward and out-
ward like chips of shattered rainbows
and will glow with love beams
shining to the ends of this universe
and lapping over to the next
shouting their joy and singing to the glory of God.

Credo

I believe the way is through the angels;
to divine guidance, to inner knowledge,
and intuition.
I believe my heart leads me to the "oneness"
to the "all that is."
I believe my love reaches beyond this Earth
spanning the universe like the rainbow rays
of the great central sun, encompassing all
and raining beams of liquid color and
vibrations of love over all of God's beautiful
thought; over all who believe and all who love.

From the Angels

You are our beloveds, precious beyond your belief.
We shield you from the demons of deceit,
We bring you light.
We bring you love.
We are the messengers.

Music of the Spheres

Help us bring to you the music of the universe.
Chords of love tones blended with
God's own breath;
His vibration of ecstasy
echoing throughout the galaxies,
singing the songs of life.

Nightlights

A million lights shine from above.
Each one expressing the love of its Creator.
Each nightlight shedding its brightness
over the Earth
while its soul-mate, the sun, sleeps.
Infinite sparkles scattered across the universe,
like handsful of tiny diamonds tossed skyward
and once thrown cling to the black velvet of space.
The moonlight breaks through its misty veil to
salute the beauty of the evening dress the night time
wears and then fades into the horizon
to make way for the splendor of the rising sun.

Star Seed

Look at the star's silvery light
pouring down and pooling at your feet.
Dip your toe into its liquid essence,
feel the beauty.
Oh Father-Mother of all
let us feel Your presence in all things of beauty.
Let us find truth as we search for the face of God

The End Times

When I look skyward I see God
in every shimmer of the red, and blue, and gold of
every one of a billion, trillion stars;
God's tapestry, embroidered with the silver threads
of his thoughts.
Perhaps the embryos of ideas
still in the womb of space,
waiting in their gestation to grow and grow
until they are expelled into a virgin galaxy
to start a new world, an infant creation,
the newborn expression of God's love.

Ammachi

Everything brings me closer to God
joining my brothers and sisters from far-flung
places of the Earth to honor a living saint.
Our skin tones blending on God's rainbow palette of
black, yellows, reds and whites; mingling our essences until
we are one body, a blessed child of
mother-father love;
A unique newborn, birthed from anxious parents
carrying the beauty of their union
in their search for the way to the Emerald Mountain
and bliss.

Star Seed

Crystal caves of healing await rediscovery.
And ruby lasers that rejuvenate damaged parts
of the body lie unused.
Walls of pure gold draw into their reflections
the dead cells of the ancients
waiting to rebuild each nucleus,
listening to hear each newborn breath
drawn from the lungs of God,
while the Emerald Mountain waits silently
for its first climber.

Star Seed

Poetry from the white light
blesses us with its pure thoughts.
Pictures painted with words
are drawn from the vocabulary of God.
And music, heard with the heart
beats to the rhythm of the universe,
touching every emotion,
wringing every chord of God's love from our being.
With perfect harmony it plucks the strings
of joy, of love, of ecstasy.

Life Cycles

How easily the fall slips into place;
A cool breeze breathing gently
over the scorched earth of summer,
while the trees dress themselves
in the hot colors of fire.
Vibrant orange and deep shades
of red and yellow
light the leaves as if in defiance
of the cooling air
and then fade and die
and fall to the breast of Mother Earth
to nourish the soil and await
the frostbite of winter.
All sleep then while they wait
for the seasons to repeat their role
and for the spring to show off her newborn.

Bimini

A playground of water
hides the Crystal City
that men built.
Buildings of clear quartz
reach for the surface with
cathedral-like spires
pointing to the heavens.
And vibrations swirl the
water in spirals of energy
that pull and draw at the
surface like invisible fingers.

A master country, designed
by a master God and meant
to last forever now lies
locked in its vault with rivets
forged by greed and peopled
by those drugged with
the power of their own conceit.

A gift from God, was this power,
to be used in co-creation
with the Oneness and with
a waste of energy and a waste
of thought this early generation
of man destroyed itself through
the misuse of the magnificent

power of knowledge laid
down for them in the Holy Hall of Records by
God himself.
But it will rise again
reaching with desperate hands
toward the surface, begging
with prayerful words for restitution and humbly
asking for absolution.

September 11, 2001

On the seventh day God rested.
And in the year two-thousand and one
the sky grew dark with smoke and death and a cry
of pain was heard across the planet
and the angels cried.

Tears of sorrow furrowed the Earth
and sadness dimmed its light
and the universe trembled.

What image of God had a man
who could cause the universe to vibrate to the
screams of his brothers and sisters and call it holy;
who could stop the Earth in its orderly turn
and call it victory?
What image should any man of spirit energy have
but compassion and love?

And on the eighth day I heard a beautiful voice
singing and I knew that he was God.

Adonai

Children of God

He dropped his thread from the grid.
With the tensile strength of silk he wound his web
around the East and the West of the globe.

From the center of this delicate network he sits
and directs his army of like spinners as they work
their smaller snares around the sleeping prey.

And once entrapped in a cocoon-like case
their victims wait and struggle to find a weakness in
their walls of silk, but the spinners are not through
with their taunts. "In the name of God, Buddha,
The Oneness, Allah, I sentence you to live."

Eternal Now

Life creeps by on ghost feet;
shadows of things done
and people met,
happy laughter and sad times,
tears shed and lessons learned
disappear with a look cast over a shoulder
and a hand flung out to grasp and hold
these smoky people and fading memories;
perhaps to be relived in some other life or
in some new time.

Star Seed

I hear your yearning
for peace and quietude
over the cacophony of
anguished sounds.
Sounds of exploding bodies
blown into atoms never
to shelter a soul again.
In the sands my son,
your brother, walked to
bring to you the message
of peace and love.

I am here. Look for me.
ask me to cleanse the
Earth of war, of hate,
of bloodshed.
Pray the vibration of the
planet to pure light.
That is where I am and
where I'll always be.

Star Seed

I have a spider on my wall.
I have asked him to leave,
told him that he does not belong in my house
and still he lingers.

Must I extinguish this small life?
Must I vanquish this tiny consciousness
and if I do what will I have gained?
If one person's death diminishes us all
then am I not diminishing his world?

The spider world is after all a part
of the scheme of things.
They help reduce the fly population.
I don't know what flies reduce if anything;
and so he clings to my wall while I ponder his fate.

I think I will just let him leave as he came,
silently and unseen.

The Separation from God

I have faint memories of God's embrace
cushioning me from the buffets
of the galactic winds; shielding me
from the fierce gusts of the hot breath of anger,
unhappiness and dissonance.
Discordant tones crying out to the Creator,
"Take me back, take me back.
Place Your golden fingers over
my bleeding wounds.
I'll be good. I'll obey. I'll be love."

Star Seed

A perfect nighttime with
crystal air so sharply clear
it seemed to cut
through the clouds with
knifelike strokes.
A three-quarter moon posed
in the center of its portrait
wearing pin-pricks of starry
light as its evening cloak;
then one of their kind moved
in erratic starts and stops
blinking on and off colors of light.
From where do you come
friends of the night?
Do you come to share the
Wondrous gift we call the "Oneness,"
The "All That Is?"
Do you come in love?

Kid Stuff

There is not much time left.
      I have to go.

"One, two, three alary
 my first name is Mary."

But time does not exist in space.

"Don't you think that I look cute?
 in my father's bathing suit?"

Then why am I in this race?

"I don't want to play in your yard,
I don't like you anymore."

Not much time left;
      keep up the pace.

"You can't shinny up my rainpipe
you can't climb my cellar door."

But look above you
      are we not in space?

Star Seed

Lives of bliss replace longing and strife.
Are you ready?
Lives of ecstasy supplant the torture of war and the longing
for the sweet scent of peace.
Do you care?
Fulfilled lives vibrating to the music of God's love await
you just a heartbeat away.
Can you hear it?
Embrace the bliss, grasp the ecstasy, listen to the music of
fulfillment for then you are home.
Are you ready?

Star Seed

Have you listened to the wind?
Then you've heard the voice of God.
Have you seen the flowers of the Earth?
Then you know his gentler thoughts.
Have you noticed the sweetness of small animals?
Then you know how much more precious
He believes His larger creation to be.
"Mankind, I made you like me.
You can make winds blow.
You can imbue the unique scents to the flowers.
You can be me."

Star Seed

"I've come to express my love for you little sister,
love for the little master on her journey,
love for the respect and appreciation
shown the Ascended Masters.
Speak to me sister.
I will hear you. I'm always near;
not much longer on your path.
We'll share the wonders that you seek;
caves of crystals called healing caves,
beautiful waters of liquid silver
that heal and wash away
the wounds and traumas of Earth's trials.
We'll see all this and more.
I come to bring peace to your heart,
peace to your consciousness for only then
can love and compassion follow."

Star Seed

Cry for the children who long for the quiet of peace;
who yearn for the sweetness of innocence;
who cry for the understanding of their torturous lives.
Why am I hungry? Why am I cold?
Why am I dirty and have nothing
with which to clean myself?
It rains and I have no roof.
It snows and I freeze until I can feel no more;
my feet are gone, my fingers are gone.
Don't cry baby brother, wake up little sister.
Our father has gone off with his gun to make peace
and grow food and to build us a roof.
The big man in his palace has told us so.
Wake up, wake up brother and sister.
I don't want to be alone.
Listen to the quiet.
It has come.
Now we'll be hungry no more and we'll feel warm
and we'll never cry again.

Star Seed

We can heal ourselves if we but knock on the door
of ancient memory and throw open the portal of our inner
consciousness to release the knowledge that flows like a
soft breeze over our bodies;
prenatal information buried beneath
the implant of forgetfulness;
waiting, waiting for the white light
to sear the impurities,
the imperfections and the false beliefs
from our consciousness.

Beaches

Molten crimson from the
core of Mother Earth bursts
through her mantle and
up through space to meet
the white light of the "Oneness."

Their energies dissolve into each
other and explode, raining
glistening sand onto the Earth
while the blue and green ocean
stretches itself to meet the shore
in frothy waves.

Drifts of wispy white
define the indigo sky
as the seabirds carve their path
through the salty air.

A pale shadow moon sits shyly
behind the clouds hiding itself
from the drama of the daylight
as it goes quietly about its
work pulling the tides high and low,
covering and uncovering the tideland.
A tranquil repose is a beach;
a spiritual calm, a balm
for the soul of humankind.

Star Seed

The great spirit of the monolith showers
shimmering energy over all its universes.
Sparkles of light glitter like pin pricks through the veil
of forgetfulness implanting its wisdom to all
who rise above the anchor of humanness;
all who dare to push through the thickened consciousness
of mankind, all who laugh at those whose purpose it is to
hold souls back from their growth, their love, and their
birthright.

Meditation with the Dolphins

They came to me in a pair the silver dolphins did.
As my brother and sister they greeted me.
With loving smiles we caressed each other and with
wordless sounds we spoke
the language of the universe.
With playful frisks and jinks we swam covering great areas
of their watery planet.
Beams of light penetrated the surface of the water
and we absorbed these energizing rays with joy
uttering gleeful sounds.
As I started for the vortex they came to wish me well on
my journey home from Sirius and told me that they had a
message for me to take back to my world.
"Send love, light and compassion to the countries of sand."

Star Seed

The night watches through
       starry eyes.
Over the children of man
       she hovers in silence.
With silver fingers she
       closes theirs to rest
their souls, to nourish with sleep.

The Flutemaker
Viewing Robert Mirabal

He calls himself a flutemaker
this native American does;
indigo music, music of colors; magical
notes rise from his hand-made instrument.
Bird music, bird tones
talking their thoughts in
whistle sounds, flute-like
duets of conversations singing
the songs of the feathered world.

And dancing colors, a
kaleidoscope of movement
and sound and stories told
to the beat of the drums to
the rhythms of the universe to
the heartbeat of the Great Spirit.

They spread great feathered wings
and fly to the top of the mountain
and wingless we climb on
uncertain feet falling on the
roughness of the path, but the
music lifts us and carries us
to the top with its powerful
vibration of tones and rhythm
and emotion.

Star Seed

Angels are wonderful things;
loving and powerful
with exquisite wings
of silver and gold and feathers that vibrate
to songs that they sing.

A magnificent chorus of
God's holy realm, gracing
the universe, definers of space
flashing like diamonds
reflecting God's face.

Star Seed

If I dip my cup into
the ocean and bring it up full,
it is still the ocean
even though it has been
separated from the whole.
This is as we are to God.

Star Seed

There are starving people
in a world of plenty. Listen.

Call me forth in the name
of suffering, of anguished cries
from pain so deep I can hear
each blood drop cry my name.

All together lift your voices
in a plea for aid; feel the
emotion so deeply that the
plea becomes a scream.

You alone can raise the
light and you together can
quiet the scream.

Star Seed

Help each other through the
heartbreak of undeserved blows.
Stand in the way of the
battering winds of loss and neglect.
Stay the hand that would
wound with the sword thrusts
of uncaring hearts.
Hold out your silver salver
of aid for those in need
are Masters who have come
to offer themselves as teachers
and should be treated as
treasures of gold and all
things precious, and of
the most wonderful of
your gifts, your love, give
it all for then you make
space in your heart for more.

Creation

When I ground myself
between the white light of the "All That Is"
and the crimson core of liquid fire
at the center of Mother Earth
I see the birth of our universe.

Through veins filled with the white light of the Father
the ruby rays of the Earth Mother connect
to form the womb that shelters and nourishes
the baby worlds until each newborn
stretches and severs the umbilical
separating each infant world from its Creator.

Each heartbeat vibrates to the rhythm of the
forming universe and with each growing pain
they create the music of the spheres
and all becomes one.

Genesis

When the Oneness and the red ray of the Earth-Mother
became one, God breathed on their union
and flesh and blood were formed.
This union of God's breath and the Earth began its rotation
slowly as the rays of gold, silver, blue,
green and all colors of the heavenly palette
entered the holographic sphere of color and
by God's intent spun violently up and out into
the universe absorbing the plan of Father-Mother
God and there began to separate into the
two natures of mankind.
When the sphere returned to the creator Earth,
man and woman departed from the hologram
and looked around in great wonder and awe,
then walked off into the garden to start their
journey towards enlightenment.

Magic

I need magic in my life;
bright and beautiful jewels
that manifest their color and
energy in rays that speak
to me in cosmic thoughts;
that teach me how to
breathe with God's lungs
for I cannot breathe otherwise,
I cannot live otherwise; and
when the journey becomes
too long and I tire, then, ah then
the greatest magic of all,
I climb the Emerald Mountain
into the arms of God
and we are one.